THE ANCIENT WORLD

ANCIENT MAYA

BY BARBARA A. SOMERVILL

CHILDREN'S PRESS®
AN IMPRINT OF SCHOLASTIC INC.
NEW YORK   TORONTO   LONDON   AUCKLAND   SYDNEY
MEXICO CITY   NEW DELHI   HONG KONG
DANBURY, CONNECTICUT

Content Consultant
Andrew Scherer, PhD
Assistant Professor of Anthropology and Archaeology
Brown University, Providence, Rhode Island

Library of Congress Cataloging-in-Publication Data
Somervill, Barbara A.
  Ancient Maya/by Barbara A. Somervill.
    p. cm.—(The ancient world)
  Includes bibliographical references and index.
  ISBN: 978-0-531-25181-2 (lib. bdg.) — ISBN: 978-0-531-25981-8 (pbk.)
 1. Mayas—Juvenile literature. 2. Mayas—Social life and customs—Juvenile literature.
3. Civilization, Ancient—Juvenile literature. 4. Mexico—Civilization—Juvenile literature.
5. Central America—Civilization—Juvenile literature. I. Title.
  F1435.S67 2012
  972'.6—dc23   2012001244

Maps by XNR Productions, Inc.

All rights reserved. Published in 2013 by Children's Press, an imprint of Scholastic Inc.
Printed in the United States of America 113

1 2 3 4 5 6 7 8 9 10 R 22 21 20 19 18 17 16 15 14 13

Humans first arrived in Mesoamerica around 21,000 years ago.

There are more than 8 million Maya living today.

JOURNEY BACK TO THE ANCIENT MAYA

Many Maya ruins, such as Chichen Itza, now draw tourists from around the world.

TABLE OF CONTENTS

A jar dating to between 200 and 500 CE

The Past Is Present

See for yourself how
the ancient Maya culture is still
present in our lives today.

*A modern recreation of
an ancient Maya mask*

PUZZLE PIECES

When the Spanish conquered the Maya in the 1500s, they did everything they could to wipe out Maya culture. They forced the Maya to become Roman

The Spanish conquistadores attacked the Maya in order to take their land and riches.

Catholics and banned traditional Maya customs and religious ceremonies. They insisted that the Maya speak Spanish. They replaced Maya nobles and warriors with Spanish governors. The Spanish destroyed written records that would have provided a more complete understanding of Maya culture. The Maya civilization was broken into a puzzle with many missing pieces. So, how do we know what we know about the Maya?

Maya **architects** produced massive **pyramids** that were as well built and enduring as those in Egypt. Spanish conquerors left great cities in ruin, but those ruins serve as evidence of what were once thriving trade centers. Palaces, temples, plazas, and roads remain as proof that kings once ruled, priests led **rituals**, citizens

architects (AHR-ki-tekts) people who design buildings and supervise the way they are built

pyramids (PIR-uh-midz) ancient stone monuments where rulers and their treasures were buried and rituals were performed

rituals (RICH-oo-uhlz) acts or series of acts that are always performed in the same way, usually as part of a religious or social ceremony

gathered together, and people traveled from one place to another. They are the first pieces of the puzzle.

When **archaeologists** began to investigate the Maya culture, they became diggers, artists, and puzzle solvers. After years of neglect, many Maya ruins had been covered over by dense jungle plants. Over the past century, archaeologists have uncovered many more ruins, and information continues to be revealed.

Art is another important piece of the great puzzle. Pottery bears decorations showing hairstyles, clothing, dances, and weapons used by the Maya. Illustrations of men dressed in leopard skin cloaks or warriors bearing spears and shields show the roles different people played in the Maya story. Carved statues, door frames, and entryways depict the gods Mayas believed in and show how kings and priests participated in religious rituals. Maya **murals**, such as the ones decorating the pyramid at Calakmul discovered in 2009, provide insight into the everyday lives of common folk.

The most difficult part of solving the puzzle has been decoding the **hieroglyphics** of **stelae** and **codices**. There are no remaining readers of the complicated Mayan language. Decoding the hieroglyphs began with the Dresden Codex, one of four surviving Maya texts. In 1832, scientist Constantine Rafinesque figured out the Maya's counting system by studying part of the Dresden Codex. Since then, scholars around the world have worked to build on Rafinesque's discoveries and uncover the meaning behind the complex Maya hieroglyphs. Their efforts have been exciting and frustrating. Just when scholars think they've fit some puzzle pieces together, they discover new errors. Even today, many more missing parts of the puzzle are needed before the full picture of the Maya civilization is revealed.

archaeologists (ahr-kee-AH-luh-jists) people who study the past, which often involves digging up old buildings, objects, and bones and examining them carefully

murals (MYOOR-uhlz) large paintings done on a wall

hieroglyphics (hire-uh-GLIF-iks) a system of writing used by ancient Mayas, made up of pictures and symbols that stand for words and syllables

stelae (STEE-lahy) upright stone slabs or pillars bearing inscriptions or designs and serving as monuments or markers

codices (KOH-dih-sees) collections of manuscript pages held together by stitching or folding; an early form of books

Scholars are still working to discover the meaning behind some Maya hieroglyphs.

CHAPTER ONE

FROM THE BEGINNING

Humans first arrived in **Mesoamerica** as early as 21,000 years ago. They were hunter-gatherers, people who traveled from place to place to find food. For them, Mesoamerica must have seemed like a paradise. Fruits, nuts, and vegetables grew throughout the year. The forests and plains were rich with birds, mammals, and insects to provide protein in their

Archaeological digs have helped us learn more about early Mesoamericans.

diets. The climate was never particularly cold, but there were times when it seemed that rain poured down without end. Still, early humans needed water, and they found it in Mesoamerican rivers, lakes, and underground streams.

There were a few drawbacks to this otherwise ideal land. Volcanoes spewed lava and hot ash on a regular basis. The ground shook from occasional earthquakes. Heavy rains brought landslides and mudslides. On the Yucatán Peninsula, the earth caved in to reveal underground pools of water. During the hottest months of the year, intense hurricanes caused floods and brought winds strong enough to fell trees.

Volcanoes were sometimes a threat to the ancient people of Mesoamerica.

Mesoamerica (mez-oh-uh-MARE-ih-kuh) the area extending from central Mexico south to Honduras and Nicaragua in which several pre-Columbian cultures thrived

COUNTING TO ZERO

Compared to most other ancient civilizations, the Maya had advanced knowledge of mathematics. While our numerical system is based on the number ten, the Maya based their system on twenty—the number of fingers and toes that humans have. Maya numbers were written using three symbols. A dot equaled one, a line equaled five, and a seashell shape equaled zero. The symbols were stacked on top of each other to form larger numbers. For example, thirteen was

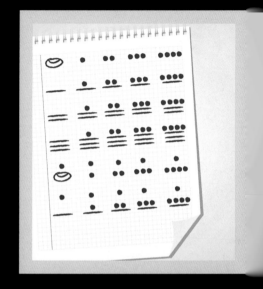

written as three dots in a row stacked on top of two parallel lines. Twenty was written as a dot above a shell.

The Maya were one of the first groups of people to understand the concept of zero, using it to record place values in numbers above nineteen. This gave them the ability to accurately record large numbers and keep track of dates. Today, zero remains a necessary part of the modern number system. Without it, we would be unable to work with any number above nine!

Between 3500 and 2000 BCE, humans began to build permanent villages in the region. These settlements formed the roots of the Maya civilization. Farmers planted crops and raised animals, mostly dogs and turkeys, which they kept in pens. They fished with nets and preserved the fish with salt for later use. Meat was cooked in stews or grilled like barbecue, and it was also smoked to be preserved for months. Strips of dry meat cured over coals tasted somewhat like beef jerky. Men made stone tools by a process called knapping, or chipping away small bits of stone. Women stored food in pottery jars or baskets, and wove cloth from cotton plants, which they grew as a crop.

Clay dishes were often painted with interesting designs.

THE PRECLASSIC PERIOD (1800 BCE–250 CE)

The Preclassic period was one of change and growth for the Maya. Small villages evolved into cities led by chiefs, who were the first members of the Maya noble classes. Chiefs served as religious leaders, **political** leaders, and warriors. They were expected to make **sacrifices**, such as cutting themselves and offering their own blood to the gods.

People paid **tribute** to their chief in the form of corn, other foodstuffs, cloth, labor, and military service. Chiefs were expected to be superior warriors themselves. They were the generals of their local armies, and success in battle was a necessary part of their leadership.

political (puh-LIT-i-kuhl) of or having to do with governments and how they are run

sacrifices (SAK-ruh-fise-ez) the offerings of something to a god or other supernatural being

tribute (TRIB-yoot) something done, given, or said to show thanks or respect, or to repay an obligation

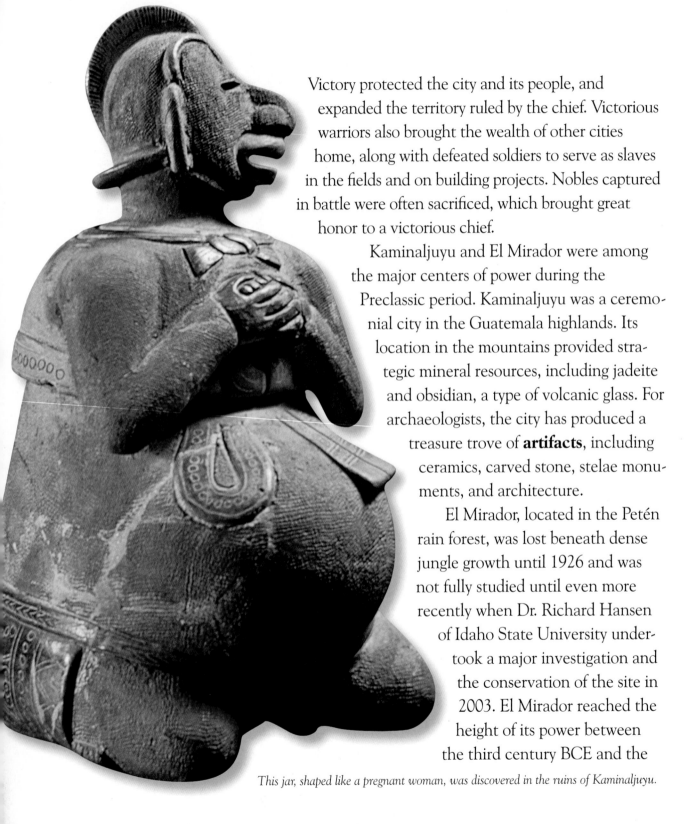

Victory protected the city and its people, and expanded the territory ruled by the chief. Victorious warriors also brought the wealth of other cities home, along with defeated soldiers to serve as slaves in the fields and on building projects. Nobles captured in battle were often sacrificed, which brought great honor to a victorious chief.

Kaminaljuyu and El Mirador were among the major centers of power during the Preclassic period. Kaminaljuyu was a ceremonial city in the Guatemala highlands. Its location in the mountains provided strategic mineral resources, including jadeite and obsidian, a type of volcanic glass. For archaeologists, the city has produced a treasure trove of **artifacts**, including ceramics, carved stone, stelae monuments, and architecture.

El Mirador, located in the Petén rain forest, was lost beneath dense jungle growth until 1926 and was not fully studied until even more recently when Dr. Richard Hansen of Idaho State University undertook a major investigation and the conservation of the site in 2003. El Mirador reached the height of its power between the third century BCE and the

This jar, shaped like a pregnant woman, was discovered in the ruins of Kaminaljuyu.

first century CE. The city's center covered about 10 square miles (26 square kilometers) and was probably home to several thousand monuments, temples, homes, and other buildings.

The Maya made significant cultural advances during the Preclassic period. They developed a system of writing, using **glyphs** to represent words. Chiefs assigned stone carvers to produce stelae as monuments to their success. The stelae stood in the central plaza for all to see, despite the fact that only a handful of people could read. Scribes wrote of a chief's heroics in codices, none of which have survived. The Maya also made great strides in mathematics and astronomy. They developed one of the first solar calendars and

Dr. Richard Hansen's (above) discoveries have helped shed light on the history of El Mirador.

artifacts (AHR-tuh-fakts) objects made or changed by human beings, such as tools or weapons used in the past

glyphs (GLIFS) written symbols used to represent spoken words

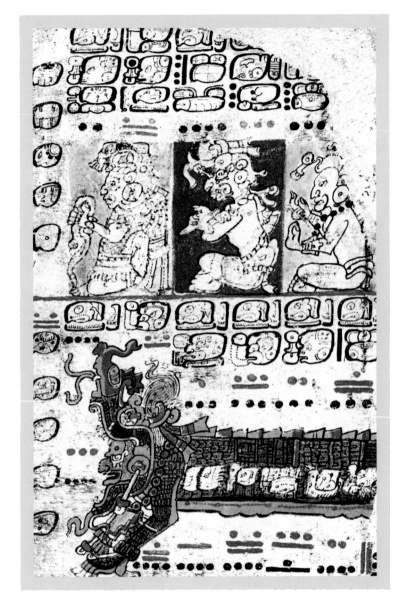

The Maya writing system was unlike most systems used today.

dynasties (DYE-nuh-steez) a series of rulers belonging to the same family

three other calendars, including the 260-day sacred calendar, called the *tzolk'in*. Each calendar had a specific use. For example, the Long Count calendar recorded all history, and the tzolk'in kept the schedule of religious events.

There was a division of labor among peasants, and the majority of people were involved in growing, fishing, hunting, and preparing food. Agriculture revolved around corn, beans, and squash. When not growing crops or hunting, men were expected to work on construction projects or train for the military.

THE CLASSIC PERIOD (250–1000 CE)

The Maya culture flourished during the Classic period. **Dynasties** ruled the major cities of Tikal, Calakmul, Yaxchilan, Palenque, Caracol, and Copan, among others. The rulers of each of these city-states tried to dominate their local regions and develop small neighboring cities to take advantage of their agriculture, quarrying, or trade. The more powerful a city's king was, the greater chance of success for its people. The trouble with dynasties, however, was that sons were not always the great leaders their fathers had been.

Tikal had one of the longest reigning dynasties, lasting through thirty-nine kings and more than eight hundred years. It began with the reign of Yax Ehb Xook circa 90 CE and continued through the reign of Jasaw Chan K'awiil II, which began around 869. Tikal had already existed for several centuries, but during the Classic period, it became one of the largest cities in the southern lowlands, with a population of possibly ninety thousand citizens.

Large cities such as Tikal were bustling centers of activity.

Tikal grew in power by defeating its neighbors in war. A successful war provided more land to grow corn, beans, and squash, as well as captives for slaves and nobles for sacrifices to the gods. Tikal's rulers watched their neighbors, waiting until a city-state looked ripe for conquering.

The nearby city-state of Calakmul saw Tikal as an enemy. Its leaders worried that they might be Tikal's next target. When Tikal conquered the neighboring city of Rio Azul, Calakmul took action. The ruler of Calakmul decided to protect his people by making treaties with Tikal's trading partners, cutting them off from Tikal one by

The ruins of Tikal stand today in what is now Guatemala.

one. When Calakmul and Caracol, another large and powerful city, joined forces, war was at hand.

Tikal attacked Caracol in 562, but could not defeat the combined forces of Caracol and Calakmul. Tikal's ruler was captured and sacrificed. That was the price of failure. For many years after this defeat, Calakmul ruled Tikal from afar, even though Tikal's ruling dynasty remained on the throne.

When Jasaw Chan K'awiil I (reigned 682–734) became Tikal's ruler, he hoped to regain the city-state's lost power. His plan took years. First, he honored Tikal's former kings, making sacrifices to the gods in their memories. He built a massive temple and trained for battle. Slowly, he reduced Calakmul's power by raiding its dependent cities. Once Calakmul was sufficiently weakened,

The ruins of Caracol are located in modern-day Belize.

19

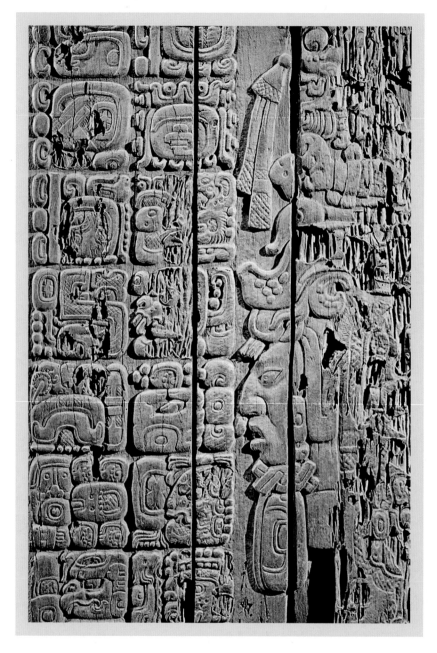

This carving was made to celebrate a victorious battle of Yik'in Chan K'awiil in 743 CE.

Jasaw Chan K'awiil invaded and captured the city-state, where he then reigned for fifty years. After his death, his son Yik'in Chan K'awiil became an equally powerful leader. However, the kingdom soon began falling apart. By 900, the jungle was already creeping in to take over the decaying remains of the once-great Tikal.

The city-state of Yaxchilan, located on the Usumacinta River, was surrounded and protected by water. The river formed a loop, and the city grew within it. Yaxchilan's strongest rulers were the Jaguar kings: Shield Jaguar the Great (Itzamnaaj Bahlam III, reigned 681–742), Bird Jaguar the Great (Yaxun Bahlam, reigned 752–768), and Shield Jaguar III (Itzamnaaj Bahlam IV, reigned 769–800). One of the main reasons for Yaxchilan's success was the practice of political marriage. It was customary for kings to marry the princesses of conquered enemies or favored allies. Maya kings often took several wives. Shield Jaguar the Great had Lady K'abal Xook as his principal wife, but he also married Lady Eveningstar, who was from Calakmul. Her presence in Yaxchilan helped ensure peace between the two city-states.

Shield Jaguar the Great is said to have received a jaguar-shaped helmet from his wife, Lady K'abal Xook.

Located in the southeastern part of Maya territory, the city-state of Copan was a rich agricultural and trading center. The founding dynasty began with K'inich Yax K'uk' Mo' (reigned 426–437). By the 700s, Copan had suffered from a series of fairly weak leaders. The solution was to form a committee of advisers, similar

Intricate carvings have been found in the ruins of Copan.

to a president's cabinet. All the members of the council were nobles. They met in a special building called a mat house, which got its name because only rulers had the right to sit on mats.

Nobles began building homes in the city, and soon Copan became dominated by expensive houses. The council members, not content to just offer advice to their king, wanted more power. Later kings became useless as the council took over the responsibilities of governing the city-state. The last notable king of Copan was Yax Pasaj Chan Yopaat (reigned 763– ca. 820).

Copan was located in what is now the country of Honduras.

The ruins of Chichen Itza are one of Mexico's most popular tourist attractions.

POSTCLASSIC MAYA

In the south and west, the powerful kings and their city-states began to wither away. Expensive, labor-intensive building projects and costly wars left the people unwilling to support the kings, priests, and temples of the past. The might of the Maya culture shifted northward to the Yucatan Peninsula.

The first major power there was Chichen Itza. The city was founded sometime between 750 and 800 by a group of people known as the Itza. Thanks to a powerful military and a strong economy, the city was able to expand rapidly over the next one hundred years. Most scholars believe that, at its height, Chichen Itza was the largest city-state in Maya history.

In addition to its famous pyramids, Chichen Itza is home to many magnificent statues and carvings.

Mayapan eventually became the major force on the Yucatan. A fairly small city, Mayapan was heavily protected from attack by a fortress wall. Other small cities grouped together to form the League of Mayapan. Together, the small city-states had a better chance to protect each other instead of constantly fighting petty wars.

Mayapan was a thriving trading center where merchants sold products such as salt and a distinctive blue coloring called Maya blue. Kings and priests used the brilliant blue dye in rituals, dyeing

Around 3,600 buildings have been discovered in the ruins of Mayapan.

or painting their skin. Salt was a product that everyone needed, and Mayapan traded it with other Mesoamerican societies. Mayapan's kings ruled the city for 260 years, but the noble class eventually weakened. In 1441, a group called the Xiu lords rose up against the last king of Mayapan, killing him and his family and burning the city to the ground.

THE SPANISH ARRIVE

In 1502, on his fourth voyage from Spain to the Caribbean, Christopher Columbus spied something that he described as "a canoe as long as a galleon." The canoe had more than forty passengers, including a pilot, paddlers, a merchant, and some servants. This was Europe's first encounter with the Maya.

The next contact between the Spanish and the Maya took place in 1511, when a small Spanish ship ran aground on a sandbar. The survivors were captured by local Mayas and became slaves or sacrifices. Only two survived: Gerónimo de Aguilar and Gonzalo Guerrero.

Christopher Columbus was one of the first Europeans to explore what are now North and South America.

Today, a statue of Francisco Hernández de Córdoba stands in the city of León Viejo, Nicaragua.

Guerrero, respected as a brave man, became a Maya warrior. Aguilar would later become a translator when other Spanish explorers arrived. The shipwrecked crew brought more than just men to the Maya, however. They also carried smallpox, which sickened and killed thousands of Maya over the next few years.

In 1517, Francisco Hernández de Córdoba led the next Spanish expedition to arrive in this area. He sailed to the Yucatan from Cuba, looking for natives he could take as slaves. Surprised to find such an advanced culture, Córdoba began trading with the natives and obtained small amounts of gold. His expedition did not fare well. In one settlement, the Maya ambushed the Spanish, attacking them with stones thrown from slings, arrows, and darts from blowpipes. Eighty Spaniards suffered wounds, and many died from infection.

Grijalva pelea con los In[dios]

Soon afterward, the governor of Cuba, Diego Velázquez, sent four ships containing 240 soldiers armed with crossbows and muskets to Maya territory. Led by Juan de Grijalva, the expedition was charged with exploration but was prepared to fight back if attacked. Grijalva's trip had mixed results. The men both traded and fought with various groups of Maya, and Grijalva returned to Cuba with a handful of gold and stories of a great empire to the west.

Juan de Grijalva and his men arrived in Maya lands prepared to do battle.

Grijalva's reports encouraged another Spaniard to pursue exploring the Yucatan. In 1519, Hernán Cortés set forth to seek his fortune. Landing to the north, he encountered the long-shipwrecked Gerónimo de Aguilar. With Aguilar's help in translating, Cortés learned of the wealthy Aztecs and set off to conquer the natives and steal as much of their gold as possible. The Spanish claimed all the land that had been home to both the Maya and the Aztec people. This land is now Mexico and Central America.

The Aztecs were conquered quickly, but the Maya were not so easy to overthrow. The Maya did not have one main leader or central village. Many of their cities were deep in jungles, reachable only by following difficult routes. The Spanish could barely endure the heat and humidity, and the mosquitoes that swarmed around them were unbearable. The men suffered from malaria and diarrhea and passed out from lack of water, but they did not give up. Whereas the Spanish conquered the Aztecs in a matter of months, their victory over the Maya took 170 years.

As soon as the Spanish had control over the region, they immediately installed their own governor and began working to eliminate Maya culture. In 1562, the Spanish bishop Fray Diego de Landa began an *auto de fé*—a work of faith—during which he destroyed Maya idols and burned forty important Maya religious texts, claiming them to be the work of the devil. Such activities eventually left the Maya culture almost completely devastated.

Over the next two hundred years, the Maya rebelled several times. In the 1600s, the Spanish government took land away from the Maya to give to the Roman Catholic Church and Spanish noblemen. The Maya were forced to work as slaves. Many barely had enough food and shelter to survive.

Hernán Cortés sought gold and land for Spain in the region that eventually became Central America.

Cortés and his men used powerful weapons to quickly defeat the Aztecs.

In 1761, revolutionary Maya leader Jacinto Canek began a violent uprising against the local Spanish government. The local Maya revered Canek, but the Spanish saw him as a disruptive troublemaker. One day, a Spanish merchant arrived in Quisteil, planning to collect some debts owed to him. Canek, always looking for a fight, confronted the man. With a group of armed Maya to back him up, Canek killed the merchant. The Spanish quickly sent forces to punish Canek and the other rebels. The Maya, however, were expecting the attack and ambushed the Spanish soldiers, killing army captain Tiburcio Cosgaya and five others.

The Spanish sent a force of five hundred armed soldiers to Quisteil to confront Canek and his fifteen hundred Maya rebels. Although outmanned three to one, the better-trained, better-armed Spanish were victorious and burned the village to the ground as payback. Canek was captured a couple of weeks later. He was tried and condemned to be "tortured, his body broken, and thereafter burned and the ashes scattered to the wind." The Spanish hoped that this severe punishment would discourage any future rebellion from the Maya.

However, the Maya fought back against their Spanish oppressors yet again when the **Caste** War of Yucatan began in 1847. By this time, the Yucatan was part of Mexico, which had declared its independence from Spain. However, Spanish people still held the most power in the country. Prior to the revolution, the Spanish had set up a social system that put themselves at the top. People of Spanish descent were next, followed by mestizos, or those who were part Spanish and part native. Relatives of the former Maya and Aztec nobles came next, and native peasants were at the bottom of the social system. Most government officials in the Yucatan at the time could trace their heritage to Spain.

caste (KAST) any class or group of society sharing common cultural features

The Spanish destroyed countless pieces of Maya artwork during their conquest.

The government and the Catholic Church controlled everything. Peasants paid heavy taxes, forcing them to live in true poverty. Minor eruptions arose between the Maya and the Mexican elite between 1839 and 1847. The major issue was that wealthy Spanish citizens held most of the land. Sugar and henequen plantations sprawled out, taking away farmland from Maya peasants. The combination of oppression, taxation, and poverty came to a head when Jacinto Pat, a Maya leader, began collecting arms and supplies for a revolution. The Maya rebels were successful at first. For a year, the Yucatan was considered separate from Mexico, and the Maya were in control. Minor battles and skirmishes continued over the next few decades, until, in 1901, Mexican troops were able to occupy Chan Santa Cruz, the stronghold of the rebels. An uneasy peace came to the Yucatan as Mexican leaders once more ruled over the remaining native people.

CHAPTER TWO

THE HAVES AND THE HAVE-NOTS

The Maya never formed a unified nation. The culture was made up of more than forty city-states, and its people spoke around seventy different languages. Each group was

Skilled craftsmen created pottery, weapons, and other useful items.

as independent of the others as the Apache were from the Sioux. However, there were many similarities between different groups of Maya. Each city-state was an agriculture-based society with its share of nobles, skilled craftsmen, **artisans**, and commoners.

Each person had an important role to play within Maya society.

THE ELITE CLASS

The elite class of the Maya included kings, their queens and children, and their relatives. Kings could have several wives, but women were not allowed to have more than one husband. The reason for this rule was that a king needed heirs, and he could

artisans (AHR-tih-zuhnz) people who are skilled at working with their hands at particular crafts

Kings and other nobles were at the top of the Maya social ladder, while common workers stood near the bottom.

only be sure that a son was truly his if his wife was his exclusively. The line of power passed from father to son, or king to prince. When there was no male heir, the family line was broken.

These nobles, who were at the top of the social ladder, had many responsibilities. The safety and welfare of their people was one of their most important obligations. Kings had to be warriors—and successful ones—to protect their people. The king and queen were the political and religious leaders of the city-state. They set an example for the people by making bloodletting sacrifices and appearing at rituals and political ceremonies.

The Past Is Present

FUTURISTIC FARMING

Water shortages were a frequent problem for the Maya. The region had a wet season and a dry season, and there was often not enough water to grow crops during the dry season. The Maya solved this problem by constructing irrigation systems. By the year 100 CE, the Maya at Edzna had finished the largest irrigation project in the Maya civilization, a canal system that covered 14 miles (23 km) and allowed people to travel in canoes along the route. The irrigation system at Edzna expanded the amount of land that could be farmed and increased crop yields.

The Maya at Edzna most likely also raised fish in large reservoirs that were part of the irrigation system. This makes them one of the earliest groups of people ever to farm fish. Today, over half of the fish eaten by people around the world come from fish farms (left).

shamans (SHAY-muhnz) healers in some traditional societies who deal with beings in the spirit world

Priests were also members of the elite. They could rule cities, preside over rituals, and read. Being able to read might not seem very significant today, but less than 10 percent of Maya citizens could read or write. Scribes and princes learned how to read and write from priests. Priests, kings, and sometimes queens were the only ones who could enter temples or preside over religious ceremonies. Many priests were **shamans** and healers. They dealt with illness through prayer, chanting, and herbal medicines. Sickness was considered to be a combination of physical, mental, and emotional problems.

Nobles showed their rank by the clothing and jewelry they wore. Among Maya nobles, it was fashionable to wear jade, quetzal feathers, and shell jewelry.

ARTISTS AND TRADESMEN

Artists and skilled tradesmen also enjoyed relatively high social status among the Maya. Artists used their talents to carve stone, tan leather, or produce dyes. Some made intricate feather headdresses or shields. Others created flower wreaths or necklaces. An expert weaver, a woman who stitched beautiful embroidery, or a person who made delicate pottery were all artisans in Maya communities.

Skilled tradesmen included jewelers, wood-carvers, and shell workers. Goldsmiths produced an array of elaborate plugs, which were pieces of jewelry worn in stretched piercings. The Maya made such piercings in their noses, ears, and lips. Many plugs were in the shapes of flowers. Since jade was worth more to the Mayas than gold, jade carvers were highly valued in a Maya community, but they worked only for nobles.

Construction projects also created a need for knowledgeable specialists. Architects designed a variety of incredible buildings,

Maya artisans wove colorful patterns into their cloth.

and expert stonecutters harvested useful building materials from quarries. Shaping the stone to construct a pyramid or a temple was difficult. The Maya decorated their buildings with intricate carvings, which required both artistic talent and years of training. The people who built the temples, pyramids, and palaces that make up the ruins we see today were highly valued members of Maya society.

The Maya included detailed carvings in their construction projects.

COMMONERS

Commoners provided the labor that fed the cities, cleared the land, and built the roads. They led fairly simple lives, and their daily activities depended on the needs of nature, their rulers, and their priests. When it was planting time, commoners worked the fields. If their rulers declared war, they served as the lowest ranking warriors. When the priests held rituals, they were expected to attend. The Maya did not run a democracy. Commoners had no vote in making laws and no say in how those laws were enforced. However, if they were unhappy with their rulers, they often chose to follow new ones instead.

Maya commoners worked hard and contributed greatly to society.

Maya women were responsible for spinning cotton into thread and yarn.

A volcanic event at Ceren has provided us with insight into how commoners lived. When a volcano erupted there, it blanketed the village with ash, preserving the homes of rulers and commoners alike. Found among these preserved ruins was an entire farming village. As excavators dug through the ash they discovered evidence that commoners lived reasonably well. Their homes were made of adobe brick and usually consisted of a single common living area rather than separate rooms. Most commoners had collections of pottery for storing, cooking, and serving food. They also had tools for grinding grain into flour and cornmeal.

If a person was born a commoner, there was little chance that he or she would ever improve in social standing. Generally, the sons of a man who farmed, dug drainage ditches, and served in the army would have the same life as their father. Women were expected to produce children, raise them, and feed the family. They also did the household's washing, weaving, gardening, and cleaning. A woman's daughters might marry and move to another household, but their responsibilities in life would largely remain the same.

CRIME AND PUNISHMENT

A person's social class determined the punishment if he or she broke community laws. Some Maya laws might seem strange today. There were punishments for commoners caught wearing green quetzal feathers or shell jewelry. Murder of a slave mattered very little, while murder of a noble was serious. The judge and jury for most crimes was the king or a group of noble officials, depending on the importance of the person accused and the crime committed. There were no lawyers to speak out in defense of the accused and no appeals of sentences.

For the crime of theft among commoners, the usual punishment was for the thief to simply give back or pay for the item stolen. Payment was made with grain, cloth, or even labor. Theft among elites was treated more harshly. If the theft was serious, the criminal's personal possessions might be sold off to repay the debt. If that wasn't enough, it was possible that the guilty party might be sold into slavery or put in jail. A thief who stole from nobles bore his crime on his face for the rest of his life. Once found guilty, his face was permanently tattooed.

Maya law punished people who harmed quetzal birds.

Death sentences were carried out on execution blocks.

Men and women were not punished equally. If a married woman had an affair with a man who was not her husband, she was humiliated in public. The other citizens in the village or city were told of her crime, and other village women shunned her. A man guilty of the same crime could be beaten or put to death.

Death sentences were common. Serious injury of a person or murder usually brought a death sentence. In the case of murder, the family of the victim could ask that the guilty party be put to death the same way their relative had been killed. As a result, the Maya had a full range of death penalty options. Stoning was popular, as was shooting by bow and arrow. Some criminals were even dismembered or beheaded. One punishment that seems especially shocking today was for the crime of killing a quetzal bird. Anyone caught killing a quetzal was put to death, with no exceptions.

CHAPTER THREE

PLAINS, FORESTS, AND PEAKS

I f you were going to travel from the northeastern tip of the Maya range to the southwestern corner, you would need to pack a lot of different equipment. Sunscreen, an umbrella, insect repellent, wading boots, a **machete**, and a winter coat

The Maya built their settlements amid vast, green forests and wide open plains.

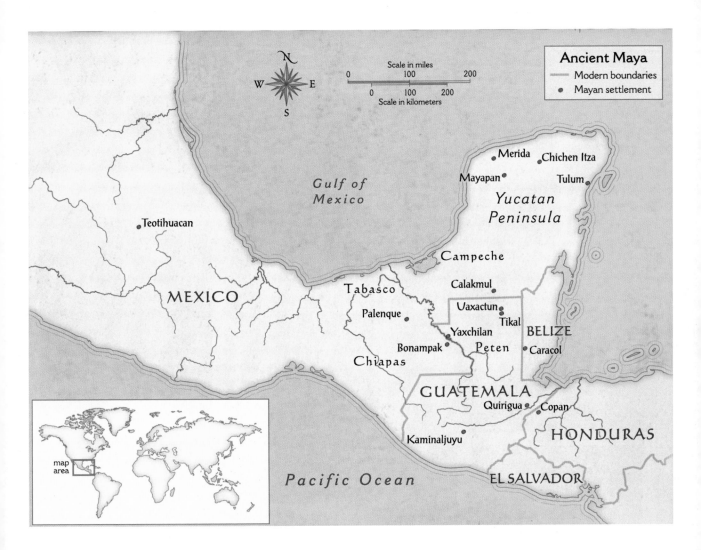

Ancient Maya
— Modern boundaries
• Mayan settlement

Gulf of Mexico

Merida • • Chichen Itza
Mayapan • Tulum •
Yucatan Peninsula

Teotihuacan •

Campeche

Tabasco

Calakmul •
Uaxactun •
Palenque • • Tikal
Yaxchilan • BELIZE
MEXICO
Bonampak • Peten • Caracol
Chiapas
GUATEMALA
Quirigua • • Copan
Kaminaljuyu • HONDURAS

map area

Pacific Ocean EL SALVADOR

would all come in handy on your journey. It would not matter what time of year you made this trek, as temperature changes in the lands of the ancient Maya depend more on altitude than on season. You can go from sweltering beaches to much cooler mountain peaks at almost any time of the year. These dramatic variations in climate and geography help explain how the Maya were able to avoid attacks from foreign armies for so many years.

machete (muh-SHET-ee) a long, heavy knife with a broad blade, used as a tool or a weapon

The Past Is Present
FLOWING BENEATH OUR FEET

In 2007, a pair of divers announced the discovery of a 95-mile-long (153 km) underground river system, interlaced with huge chambers and narrow tunnels. Considered the longest underground river system, the Sac Actun system passes under the surface of the Yucatan Peninsula. Divers Stephen Bogaerts and Robbie Schmittner made five hundred dives over four years into the Sac Actun before the final dive that revealed the full extent of the river.

The Maya relied on the Sac Actun and other underground rivers as a source of freshwater for drinking and watering crops. Today, that same water system is an important source of fresh water for the local tourism industry. Many people also visit the rivers to dive and explore these unique aquatic environments. Bogaerts warns, however, that the system is vulnerable to contamination. "These cave systems are so extensive and so interconnected that if there is a point of pollution in one area then it can quickly get distributed to a very, very wide area," he says.

The Yucatan

On the surface, the Yucatan Peninsula seems to be flat and featureless. There are no large lakes, rushing rivers, or tall mountains. The soil is shallow and lacks the richness needed for growing plentiful crops. Yet the Maya found this an ideal place to live. Chichen Itza, Tulum, Coba, Uxmal, and a dozen other major Maya cities thrived on the Yucatan.

The surface land may not look like much, but mysterious geography lies hidden beneath the peninsula's surface. Twisting underground rivers flow slowly toward the sea. Wide underground lakes lie trapped between layers of limestone. At times, the limestone on

Huge underground lakes were a useful water source for the Maya.

cenotes (seh-NOH-tayz) sinkholes or naturally forming wells, formed by the collapse of surface limestone

the surface cracks and caves in to the underground water, creating natural wells. These wells, called **cenotes**, provided freshwater to the Maya and were occasionally used for religious offerings. The word *cenote* comes from the Yucatec Maya language and refers to any location with accessible groundwater.

Yucatan plant life is a mix of low-lying tropical shrubs, henequen, *caoba*, cedar, and ceiba. Henequen was the "green gold" of the Yucatan for the Maya. This useful plant provided fiber to make rope and twine. Caoba is a type of mahogany that was used

Henequen is still grown and harvested in some parts of Central and South America.

to make doors and furniture. Cedar is a member of the pine family and was used to repel insects. Among the Maya, the ceiba tree was revered for its gifts of wood, silky cotton fibers, and beautiful flowers.

Native to the Yucatan are many animals that the Maya hunted for food, fur, feathers, and skins. The jaguar was the Yucatan's largest predator. Both jaguars and humans fed on flamingos, quail, ducks, and tapirs. The paca, a large rodent similar to a guinea pig, was a popular source of meat and often wound up in Maya stews and roasting pots. The Maya also hunted animals such as deer, peccaries, iguanas, turtles, and wild turkeys for food. Not quite as easy to handle, but still a common source of meat, were crocodiles and several dozen varieties of snakes. While many of the Yucatan's snakes are not venomous, the region is home to rattlesnakes, coral snakes, pit vipers, and the deadly fer-de-lance.

The Maya hunted tapirs as a source of meat.

THE PETEN

The Peten region of Guatemala is a dense rain forest with tall trees, thick underbrush, and an exceedingly wet, sticky climate. The Maya built many large cities in the Peten, including Tikal, Yaxha, Naranja,

The Maya admired jaguars for their remarkable hunting skills.

and Piedras Negras. Two major rivers, the Usumacinta and the Pasión, intersect in the Peten at the site of Altar de Sacrificios, one of the Maya civilization's most important trading centers.

The Peten is a land of tall hardwood trees, many of them covered with strangler vines and exotic flowers. Orchids grow wild, lighting the shadowy jungles with bright pinks, yellows, and deep purples. The Maya used many of the local plant species as medicines. They used the *chaya* plant for its rich vitamin content and the bark of the *balché* tree to treat wounds and heal damaged muscles.

The Maya of the Peten dealt with swarms of mosquitoes, scorpions, centipedes, and beetles. Jaguars, pumas, ocelots, margays, and jaguarundis prowled through the dense jungle as howler monkeys shrieked from the canopy above. Tiny, agile spider monkeys competed with macaws and parrots for fruit and nuts to eat. Camouflaged against the vivid greens of the plant life, a boa constrictor might have sunned itself while iguanas watched carefully from tree branches above the forest floor. The Maya jungle had more than 8,000 species of trees, vines, shrubs, and wildflowers. Eight hundred species of birds shared the forest with millions of insects and 250 species of mammals.

The lowland jungles were excellent locations for Maya villages. They provided ample food and water, and the climate, although wet, was mild with fairly even temperatures throughout the year.

Up on the Mountaintop

The Maya territory was bordered by mountains to the west in what is now Chiapas and to the east in what is now Belize. The Guatemalan highlands are the result of millions of years of volcanic activity. The threat of eruptions and being engulfed in clouds of ash did not seem to worry the Maya. They settled near such

Boa constrictors rely on their coloring to help them stay hidden from potential prey.

sites as Volcán de Fuego, which frequently erupted, releasing thick clouds of ash. The city of Ceren flourished in the shadow of the Loma Caldera volcano.

The Crystalline Mountains are the oldest rock deposits in Central America. These mountains, along with the Cuchumatanes and the Sierra de las Minas, are rich with minerals and semiprecious gems such as serpentine, blue nephrite, and jade. The mountains were also an excellent source of basalt, which was used for building and grinding stones, and gold and copper ore. Highland Maya also traded these gems and minerals for necessary goods, such as salt.

Volcán de Fuego is still active today.

The mountainsides were lush with thorn forests, tropical rain forests, and cloud forests. These woodlands sheltered such animals as red brocket deer, howler monkeys, and tapirs. Wild cats, including jaguars, cougars, onzas, ocelots, and margays, were the top predators of the region.

UP IN THE AIR

At the height of the Maya civilization, harpy eagles zoomed through the dense rain forest. Ocellated turkeys gobbled seeds from the forest floor. The horned guan, similar to a wild turkey, lit up the forest with its red legs, yellow bill, and glossy black feathers. Hidden by the mists of the cloud forest, the quetzal displayed its lush green feathers to attract a mate. While these birds came from very different habitats, they were all among the many bird species that lived on the land of the Maya.

Ocellated turkeys live almost exclusively on the Yucatan Peninsula.

The marshes, wetlands, and estuaries of modern-day Guatemala, Belize, and the Yucatan provided ideal nesting grounds for wading and waterbirds. Flocks of pink flamingos dipped their beaks into the water to strain tiny shrimp. They shared the grassy marshlands with storks, herons, cranes, and

Ceiba trees produce beautiful, brightly colored flowers.

egrets. These large birds provided a valuable source of meat, as they were easy for the Maya to hunt with blowpipes.

LIFE-GIVING PLANTS
Local plants provided the ancient Maya with wood for housing and fires, fruit and nuts for food, natural medicines, and floral beauty. In the rain forests, tall, thin ceiba trees rose 130 to 230 feet (40 to 70 meters) above the forest floor. Strangler fig vines twined their way skyward, cutting off the life of host trees.

The forests were home to many varieties of trees that the Maya used for building, toolmaking, and firewood. Sapodilla wood was soft and easily carved when first cut, but as hard as iron after it dried out. Logwood, hard as rock when it was cut down, made good foundations for buildings but was difficult to work with. Mahogany, a dark hardwood, was strong but easily worked. It was ideal for making tables, stools, and other furniture. While common people did not have much furniture, nobles often owned benches, tables, and chairs. Other trees were burned to produce charcoal, the fuel for Maya cooking fires.

In addition to being a source of wood, sapodilla trees produce edible fruit.

CHAPTER FOUR

CORN IS LIFE

Each year, as the dry season approached its end, Maya farmers began clearing new land to plant maize. They used the slash-and-burn method—they cut plants close to the root, waited for the dead plants to dry, and burned the dried leaves and stems. This provided two good results. Not only was the land cleared for planting crops, but the ash from the cleared plants nourished the soil. Corn grew well in this fertile soil, and for the Maya, corn was life. This was true two thousand years ago, and it is still true today.

Once the land was cleared, the soil had to be worked. With no large beasts to pull plows, the Maya relied on the only labor they had—themselves. They dug and hoed the soil, forming ridges and **furrows**. Using a stick, a hole was placed every few feet along each ridge, and maize seeds were dropped in and covered. Farmers used the same process to plant squash and beans in the same fields where they grew corn. This was an incredibly efficient use of the land. The cornstalks acted as poles to support the beans, and the squash leaves created shade that held water in the soil. The three crops provided a well-rounded diet for the farmer, his family, and his noble lord.

Maya men were responsible for raising crops, but they were not the society's only food providers. Women kept kitchen gardens where they grew herbs such as epazote and fruit such as tomatoes, chili peppers, gourds, and agave. They also collected fruits and nuts from the nearby forests. Many Maya had small orchards for growing papaya, avocado, guava, and cacao. *Ramón* trees provided bread nuts, which, when dried, could be ground into flour to make a flat bread similar to tortillas.

Corn was the Maya's main staple food.

furrows (FUR-ohz) the long, narrow grooves that a plow cuts in the ground

Hunters used blowpipes to kill quail, partridge, and ducks, and even howler and spider monkeys. Spears and arrows felled deer, crocodiles, manatees, tapirs, and peccaries. Traps snagged turtles and iguanas. Along the coastline, fishermen used nets, hooks, and lines to bring in shrimp, lobsters, crabs, and finfish, such as sharks, dogfish, or killifish. Fish was often smoked or salted to preserve it for eating later. Back home, in the kitchen garden, women kept caged turkeys or deer to fatten up for a feast.

Blowpipes allowed Maya hunters to shoot darts at their prey.

FANTASTIC FOOD

Corn was the main source of nutrition for the ancient Maya and is still the staple food of Central America. Central American recipes for corn and cornmeal number in the hundreds. Corn is eaten grilled on the cob, freshly cut, and in salads, soups, and stews. Cornmeal is the primary ingredient in tortillas (bottom left) and tamales.

The Maya method of processing corn required a grindstone (metate) and a hand stone (mano). The metate was a smooth slab, usually with a gentle depression in the middle. The mano was a cylindrical rock, much like a rolling pin. The Maya put grain in the metate and, using a smooth, even motion, ground it into flour by rolling the mano over it. This process also worked with cacao beans, bread nuts, peppers, and dried herbs. The Maya of Guatemala still use the metate and mano for grinding corn today.

Large containers were used to store corn and other foods.

Once the crops were brought in, the women spent time drying and processing grains, seeds, nuts, herbs, and peppers. Corn was, by far, the most important grain. Dried kernels were stored in pottery jars, baskets, or hollowed out gourds.

Food

The average Maya family ate some form of corn three times a day. Breakfast and lunch were often corn porridge, called *atole*. The runny porridge was eaten warm in the morning and cold at noon. With a consistency similar to that of a smoothie, atole could be mixed with roasted pumpkin or squash seeds, cacao, honey, or herbs. Nobles enjoyed atole with chocolate, but peasants flavored theirs with ground chilies.

Chili peppers provided the Maya with a source of strong flavors for their cooking.

The main meal of the day for Mayas was a hot dinner. This could be stew or tamales, depending on the availability of food. Tamales consisted of finely ground cornmeal, herbs, chili sauce, and usually beans. Women made a paste of the ingredients, wrapped portions in dried cornhusks or avocado leaves, and baked them in the cooking fire. Stews contained fresh meat, nuts, vegetables, and, of course, corn.

Preserving food was a challenge. Maya women learned to cut thin strips of meat and smoke it over fires to preserve it. Some fruits, such as papaya and pineapple, could be cut and dried. Others, such as avocado, had to be eaten when ripe.

FAMILY

When a Maya woman gave birth, the first thing she did was bathe her baby, then she strapped it to a board. Another board was then strapped to the baby's forehead, changing the shape of its soft head. This practice gave the child a flat, sloped forehead, assuring that it would be considered beautiful among the Maya.

Baby names were not assigned by parents. In some Maya cultures, the baby would be named after its birth date on the Long Count calendar. In other cultures, the local shaman chose a name based on predictions of the child's future.

The family lived together as a unit until its children reached adulthood. Children were considered adults once they had gone through puberty. This was an important step for young men and women. It meant they were responsible for supporting themselves and their families. Young women continued to live with their parents until they married, at about age twenty. Young men moved into a boys' dormitory. They were still expected to help their

Tamales are still a popular food in many parts of the world.

Ball games were a popular way for young Mayan men to enjoy themselves after a hard day's work.

fathers in the fields or with other jobs, but they had a looser, more entertaining life than young women. After work, young men drank and gambled and often played ball games among themselves.

Our only knowledge of marriage among the Maya comes from the records of early colonial times, some seven hundred years after the end of the Classic period. During this era, marriage was arranged

by a third party. There was no dating, courting, or long engagement. It was important that marriages did not take place between close relatives, so the family lines of the bride and groom were studied to make sure they were not related. Ideally, the bride and the groom came from the same city, as the nobles did not want to lose their workers to other towns. Noblemen, on the other hand, often married noblewomen from other city-states to build alliances between the two cities.

Newly married commoners lived with the bride's family for six or seven years after getting married. The husband worked for the bride's father as a means of paying for his bride. After that, the husband built a hut near his parents and shared the work on his father's land. All valuable goods were passed from fathers to sons. Women owned nothing.

There was much work for a family to do. They had to plant, raise, and harvest crops. Because they had idle time between planting and harvesting and during dry periods when no crops grew, most men also

Some Maya men took secondary jobs as stone carvers.

had secondary jobs. Common secondary jobs included cutting stone, laying roads, and mining jade. Most men also trained as warriors. Farming fathers trained their sons to be farmers. The sons followed their fathers' footsteps in secondary jobs as well.

Women kept the house clean, prepared food, tended the kitchen garden and animals, and raised the children. Mothers taught their daughters about food processing, weaving, gathering food, and keeping a tidy home.

WHAT TO WEAR

Only Maya nobles had a wide selection of clothing and jewelry. The type of cloth, its color, and accessories indicated the status of the wearer.

Maya children went naked until they were five years old. At that point, the boys were given loincloths and the girls were given skirts. Clothing was not formfitting or tight, but loose and flowing. Women wove the cloth from maguey fibers or cotton. They used natural vegetable dyes to produce reds, blues, greens, and yellows, dyeing the yarn first and then weaving patterns into the cloth.

Men wore cloaks or cloth tied like a loose jacket. They knotted cloth between their legs for **breechcloths** or tied it around their hips like a kilt. The clothing of artisans and lesser nobles was sometimes decorated with colorful feathers. Men also decorated themselves with nose or ear plugs, necklaces, and bracelets. In general, men wore more jewelry than women, and nobles wore more jewelry than peasants. Nobles treasured jewelry made of jade, serpentine, and exotic shells.

Women often wore a loose blouse called a *huipil*. This garment was made by cutting a head hole into a length of cloth.

breechcloths
(BREECH-klawths)
clothing worn around
the loins and buttocks

Nobles often wore elaborate, brightly colored clothing.

Face paint, as shown here in a modern reenactment, helped Maya warriors appear more threatening to their enemies.

Many women wore several layers of clothing, such as a blouse under a jacket or a skirt over a short sarong. They also enjoyed elaborate hairstyles. Women worked their long hair into braids, which they wrapped in turbans or lengths of cloth. Noblewomen tended to have much fancier hairdos than common women.

The Maya often painted their bodies or gave themselves tattoos. A tattoo design was painted on the body and then cut into the skin. Paint was mixed into the wound, and the combined scar and paint formed the tattoo. This was exceedingly painful, and tattoos were considered symbols of bravery. Not all tattoos were a sign of beauty or bravery, however. A nobleman caught stealing was forced to have his entire face tattooed as punishment.

Warriors painted their bodies to make themselves look fierce. They painted their bodies or faces with black or red paint, lined their eyes with black, and probably looked horrifying to their enemies. Priests wore blue body paint, and women painted their faces with red to make themselves more attractive.

Warriors wore jewelry and other decorative objects.

Adobe walls helped keep the interiors of Maya homes cool in hot weather.

Good Health

The Maya were remarkably clean. At a time when many Europeans avoided bathing, washing their hair, or brushing their teeth, the Maya did all three. They regularly washed in cold water. Mayas also rinsed their mouths out with water after eating and washed their hands.

Most Maya women had a basic understanding of medicinal herbs, which they used when people were sick or injured. They dosed the patient with herbal tea and hoped for the best. If a person was extremely sick, a shaman was called in. Using a combination of chanting, herbal medicine, and magic, the shaman was believed to help people expel the evil spirits causing the illness. It was common medical practice to bleed out the affected body part if herbs did not work. For example, a shaman dealt with a headache by bleeding the forehead.

Homes

Most Maya families lived in small, rectangular huts made of adobe and thatched with palm leaves, reeds, or branches. Adobe was mud formed into bricks and baked in the sun. Mud was also added in clumps to fill in the gaps in structures made of sticks. More sticks were woven to form an angled roof. Most farmhands were able to build and repair homes.

Some farmworkers also worked on other construction projects. Maya palaces and temples were made of stone. On the Yucatan, the stone was usually limestone, which was plentiful. In the highlands, basalt and lava rock were common. Building a structure of stone, particularly without beasts to haul the stone or construction equipment to lift it, required careful planning. Every Maya city had

Limestone remains a popular building material today.

at least one skilled architect who designed palaces and temples. Quarry workers cut and shaped stone for building. Farmworkers supplied the labor to erect the buildings. Because each stone used in building a pyramid weighed several tons, building was a tough job.

The Maya had a very practical outlook on life. Men expected to work the land, provide labor for buildings, and fight battles when the ruler decided to go to war. Women knew they would clean, cook, weave, and sew. They expected to marry and have children. When they died, most Maya were buried beneath the earthen floors of their huts.

Many laborers worked together to construct the Maya's incredible temples.

77

CHAPTER FIVE

REVERENCE FOR THE GODS

According to the Quiché Maya, the creation of the world depended on two forces, the sky and the water. The gods of creation simply breathed the word *earth* for land to appear. They thought of mountains and valleys, trees and vines, and it all came to be. The gods wanted beings that would praise them and revere them, as well as look after their creation, the earth. Tepeu, the Maker, and Gucumatz, the Plumed Serpent, began by making all the animals that roamed the earth, from the jaguar to the birds of the sky and the fish of the sea. But these creatures could not worship the gods.

Tepeu and Gucumatz then tried to create human beings. They were not successful at first. The earliest humans were made of clay. They could do nothing and crumbled apart. The gods, fed up with their clay humans, sent a flood to wash them away. The second group of humans they created were wooden figurines, empty-headed, and unable to revere the gods who made them. Angered by the inability of the wooden beings to praise the gods, Huracan, the god of storms, sent a flood to destroy them. The flood was not enough, so the gods asked the animals to destroy what was left.

Gucumatz may have been based on the Aztec god Quetzalcoatl.

The Past Is Present

STORMY WEATHER

When a great storm came upon the Maya, they prayed to the god Huracan to ease his anger and stop the wind and rain. He was the creator god who lived among the mists and appeared to many as wind. When the gods became angry with humans, it was Huracan who released the wind and rain that became the flood that destroyed all.

Today, the Maya god lends his name to the destructive storms—hurricanes—that so ferociously attack the land where the Maya live. Today, there are around nine of these powerful storms each year. They start in the Pacific Ocean or in the Atlantic Ocean off the coast of Africa. Similar storms in other places are called cyclones or typhoons.

In the next attempt at making humans, the animals on Earth brought ears of white and yellow corn to the gods. The goddess Xmucane ground the white and yellow corn together nine times to create living humans. This was how the Maya believed the world they knew was created. Corn was life for the Maya. It was only natural for them to believe that, since corn gave life, life came from corn.

THE GODS

The Maya had a different god for every aspect of life. They believed that gods controlled the sun, moon, and stars. The gods decided whether corn grew tall or withered in the fields. Health, happiness, and security of all depended on the moods of the gods. The Maya had more than 150 gods in their **pantheon**. Much of the information about the gods was lost as Maya texts were destroyed over time. Before scholars knew how to read Maya hieroglyphs, they recognized that specific symbols referred to specific gods. They named the gods letters of the alphabet. The letters did not indicate the gods' importance to the Maya, but the order in which scholars identified them.

The Upperworld, or the heavens, was the arena of the gods. The Maya believed the heavens were divided into thirteen layers. The layers were not separate but woven together into one realm. The Upperworld was the home to the sun, moon, and stars. The Maya were active stargazers. They watched the movement of constellations and recognized the appearance of planets in the night sky. The Maya believed that these movements indicated the feelings of the gods. For example, Maya astronomers tracked the rise of Venus in the night sky. No military ruler would have launched a battle unless Venus was in the right spot in the sky.

pantheon (PAN-thee-ahn) the gods of a particular mythology grouped together

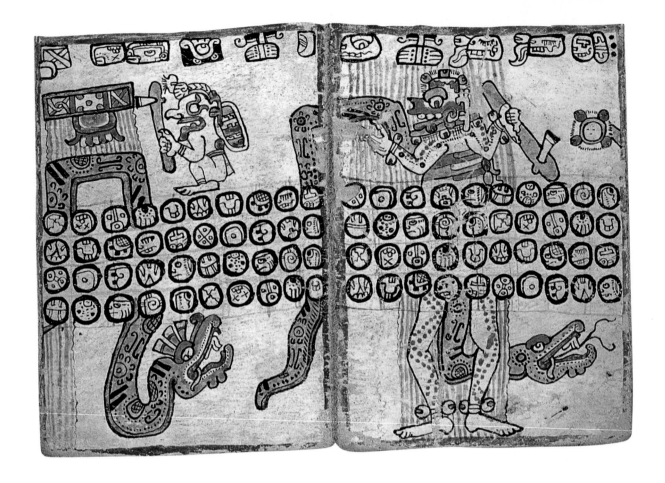

Few Maya religious texts survive today.

One of the most important gods of the Upperworld was K'inich Ajaw. He was connected to the rising sun and was the father of Itzamná, god of writing and books. The Maya believed that Chaac, the rain god who looked pretty much like a reptile, lived in caves because caves were damp. Clouds, mist, thunder, and lightning were Chaac's weapons. Tepeu, the maize god and creator god, helped form the earth and its plants and animals.

Gods had more power than goddesses. One exception was the goddess Ixchel, seen as a maiden and mother. She was the goddess of waters, the earth, and the moon. Weavers, artisans, and pregnant women all prayed to her. Ixchel was sometimes represented

This modern statue depicts Ixchel, one of the most powerful Maya goddesses.

as the moon or a rainbow, or with snakes twined through her hair, bones decorating her skirt, and claws for hands and feet. She was also the goddess of war.

According to the Quiché, the Underworld, or Xibalba, was organized into nine levels, each with its own god. These gods controlled death, disease, and evil. The Maya feared the Underworld, a dark place for people who died peaceful deaths. The Underworld was reached by water, and two great rivers flowed through it.

Among the major gods of the Underworld were Ah Pukuh, Hun Came, Vucub Caquix, and Kimi. Ah Pukuh and Kimi were death gods for the Quiché Maya. Among some Maya, they were the same god. They were depicted as skeletons with deathly eyes. The Underworld gods were often shown sitting on thrones made of bones.

Connecting the heavens and the Underworld was the World Tree, the ceiba. The tree's roots extended deep into all nine layers of the Underworld. Its trunk was firmly set on the middle world, the earth where the Maya lived. Its branches stretched into the heavens above, reaching the Upperworld. There was no one specific ceiba tree that was the World Tree, but rather every ceiba, tall and strong, held that position among the Maya.

THE HERO TWINS

One of the favorite legends of the Maya was the story of the Hero Twins. There are many tales of these two men who defeated death. In one tale, the twins are named Hunahpu and Xbalanque. They are challenged to a ball game by gods of the Underworld. The twins believe they can fool death and win the game. They agree to the game, but the gods trick Hunahpu and cut off his head. He

still tries to compete, using a squash for a head. The gods then surprise Xbalanque and Hunahpu by presenting Hunahpu's head as the ball for the game. Xbalanque fixes his brother's head back on his neck, and the twins win the ball game.

The Hero Twins were among the most beloved characters of Maya legend.

Hunahpu and Xbalanque defeated many foes throughout their adventures.

The Hero Twins had courage, loyalty, and intelligence. These were characteristics admired by the Maya, and the legends continue to be told to Maya children today.

THE RITUALS

The Maya held complicated rituals involving praying, singing, dancing, and sacrifices. Bloodletting was part of the rites of sacrifice. Nobles and priests were expected to cut themselves or pierce their bodies to honor the gods. Piercing ears and tongues were significant. By piercing the ears, the Mayas opened themselves to hearing the gods. Piercing the tongue, particularly with thorns, allowed priests to speak the words the gods spoke to them.

Bloodletting was not limited to men. Noblewomen were also expected to undergo painful sacrifices. These sacrifices were held to honor the rise of a husband to ruler, a major victory in battle, or the birth of the heir to the throne. In one carved work in

In this carving, Bird Jaguar stands above a war prisoner.

Yaxchilan, the Lady K'abal Xook is depicted performing just such a sacrifice. She appears to be pulling a rope embedded with thorns through her tongue. Her husband, Itzamnaaj Bahlam III, stands over her while her blood drips onto a piece of cloth or paper.

Animals were sometimes sacrificed to the gods.

Unfortunate captives were often the victims of Maya sacrifices.

The Maya believed blood was a sacred substance, but life was the most sacred. In addition to bloodletting, the Maya practiced human sacrifices. Peasants who were taken in battle often became slaves, but nobles or warrior chiefs were held for special religious events. The sacrifice of a peasant was worthless. Only the sacrifice of noble life would please the gods. After praying and dancing, a priest cut off the victim's head or removed the heart while the victim was still alive.

The End of Life

The Maya believed that each human being had several souls. When a body died, some of the souls also died. Other souls remained with the body, so that when the person was reborn, the human would still have a soul. Warriors who died in battle, women who died in childbirth, and people who committed sacrificial suicides to the gods went immediately to the Upperworld. Everyone else went to the Underworld to await rebirth. Dead people were buried with items that would help them in the journey to their next life. The wealthier or more important the person had been in life, the more items were buried with the body.

Commoners were usually buried under the earthen floors of their huts. Only nobles received fine burials. In the past century, archaeologists realized that some of the pyramids in Maya ruins were tombs of nobles. When tombs were opened, the archaeologists discovered bodies carefully prepared for the afterlife. The dead had been given every opportunity to rise again, to be reborn with the rising sun. Rulers went to the afterlife with rich cloth, jewelry, and symbols of their power.

Kings were often buried with jewelry and other valuable items.

CHAPTER SIX

THE MAYA TODAY

*W*e are not myths of the past, ruins in the jungle or zoos.
We are people, and we want to be respected, not to be
victims of intolerance and racism.

Rigoberta Menchú Tum
Modern-day Maya political activist

Today, many descendants of the ancient Maya live throughout North and South America.

Though it came close, the Maya culture did not disappear completely after the Spanish invasion. Today, there are more than seven million Maya living in Belize, Guatemala, Honduras, and Mexico. Another one million live in the United States. They do not live in city-states run by kings, but in towns and cities run by elected officials. They are weavers and farmers, as well as doctors, lawyers, teachers, and construction workers. Some speak Spanish and follow the Roman Catholic Church as their ancestors did after the Spanish conquest. But many speak a version of the Mayan language and practice rites and traditions of their people.

Some modern Maya continue to harvest corn, just as their ancestors did thousands of years ago.

Maya make up about two-thirds of the population of Guatemala.

Devout Maya continue to worship the gods in the mountains and in cave shrines. They sacrifice chickens and burn candles to honor the old ways. The people follow a 260-day sacred calendar, which is kept, as it was 1,000 years ago, by a shaman or "daykeeper."

The ancient Maya culture depended on corn as the staple food for existence. This has not changed. Maya farmers raise corn in fields that they clear using the same slash-and-burn method that their ancestors used. They still eat corn three times daily, usually in the form of tortillas or corn mash.

In Guatemala, government officials have oppressed the Maya for many years. By the late 1900s, thirty-five years of civil war had created a difficult atmosphere for the Maya to live in.

The Past Is Present
NATIVE TONGUES

Many descendants of the ancient Maya continue to practice the traditions and follow the lifestyles of their ancestors. As a result, the ancient Mayan language continues to thrive today in certain parts of the world. In Mexico, large groups of Maya live in the states of Yucatan, Campeche, Quintana Roo, Tabasco, and Chiapas. Many speak Yucatec Maya, and Spanish is their second language. In Guatemala, many Maya speak the dialects such as Kakchiquel, Q'eqchi, and Quiché.

The language and art of the Quiché have been preserved through the *Popol Vuh*, an important religious text, and through dramatic works such as *Rabinal Achí*, a mixture of music, dance,

and text that dates back to the fifteenth century. The *Rabinal Achí* is still performed during a special celebration each year in the town of Rabinal, Guatemala. Dancers wear elaborate costumes and tell the tale of conflict between two groups of ancient Maya.

The Guatemalan army drove farmers from their land so that wealthy companies could produce crops for export. Many Maya joined **guerrilla** groups that battled against the government to retake this land.

Rigoberta Menchú Tum, a Quiché Maya, was born and raised in Guatemala. She has worked for women's rights since her teen years, despite government opposition. Menchú joined the Committee of the Peasant Union (CUC) when she was twenty to get equal rights for Maya peasants who were abused by the Guatemalan government. After the Guatemalan army killed her brother and father, Menchú became increasingly active in organizing farmworkers and protesting government oppression. A fighter for equality for native people, Menchú was awarded the Nobel Peace Prize in 1992. In 1995, the Guatemalan government officially granted the Maya equal rights under the law.

Rigoberta Menchú Tum has helped raise awareness about the poor treatment of Maya by the Guatemalan government.

The Maya culture was never a single people with one leader and one language. The people came from different groups and spoke different languages. Today, there are about thirty different groups of Maya. The Maya remain the single largest native group in Central America, with traditions reaching back several thousand years. Many have also emigrated to North America and Europe. They carry on lives very different from their ancestors, yet they are linked by their heritage to the past.

Many Maya continue to celebrate many of the traditions of their ancestors.

BIOGRAPHIES

JACINTO CANEK (1731–1761) led the Maya on the Yucatan in a rebellion against the Spanish government. He was killed by the Spanish in retaliation for the rebellion.

CHAK TOK ICH'AAK I (REIGNED 360–378 CE) was a warrior and a ruler of the city-state of Tikal.

FRANCISCO HERNÁNDEZ DE **CÓRDOBA** (1475–1526) is generally considered the first European to explore the Yucatan Peninsula, although two earlier expeditions shipwrecked on the coast. Córdoba's expedition was not much more successful. He described the venture: "It had become obvious that we were merely wasting our time."

ITZAMNAAJ BAHLAM III (REIGNED 681–742 CE) became ruler of Yaxchilan at about age thirty-four. A warrior, he is said to have led his troops into battle in his eighties. He died at age ninety-five.

JASAW CHAN K'AWIIL I (REIGNED 682–734 CE) ruled in Tikal. By the time he took over the throne, Tikal was already in decline as a regional power.

LADY **K'ABAL XOOK** (?–729) was the principal wife of the ruler Itzamnaaj Bahlam III. Lady K'abal Xook appears in several texts in the act of performing ritual sacrifices.

Itzamnaaj Bahlam III

K'INICH HANAB PAKAL, OR PAKAL THE GREAT (REIGNED 615–683 CE) ruled Palenque for most of his eighty years, beginning his reign at about age twelve. Palenque was a major city-state during his reign in the Classic period.

K'INICH YAX K'UK' MO' (REIGNED 426–437 CE) ruled Copan, a major center in the mountains of present-day Honduras.

FRAY DIEGO DE **LANDA** (1524–1579) was the Spanish bishop of the Yucatan after the conquest was complete. He was personally responsible for the destruction of much Maya art and many Mayan books.

RIGOBERTA **MENCHÚ** TUM (1959–) is the winner of the Nobel Peace Prize for her efforts on behalf of the native people of Guatemala. She is a member of the Quiché culture of Mayas.

YAJAW TE' K'INICH II (REIGNED 553–593 CE) was a ruler of Caracol. Like many lords of his time, he had several monuments carved in his honor.

LADY **YOHL IK'NAL** (REIGNED 583–604 CE) was the only woman to rule a Maya city-state for a lengthy period. Lady Yohl remarried in order to produce an heir to the throne of Palenque.

Rigoberta Menchú Tum

TIMELINE

3114 BCE:
The world is created, according to Maya mythology. The first day of the Long Count calendar takes place in midsummer.

21,000 BCE   **3000 BCE**   **1000 BCE**

21,000 BCE:
The first hunter-gatherers settle in the region that will be home to the Maya.

600 BCE:
The Maya begin digging irrigation canals to increase crop yields.

400 BCE:
The earliest known solar calendars come into use by the Maya.

300 BCE:
Kings and chiefs are selected to rule Maya cities and towns.

683 CE:
The ruler Pakal the Great dies in the city of Palenque.

751 CE:
Alliances among Maya city-states begin to break down. Cities come into conflict over land and wealth.

869 CE:
Tikal reaches its peak and begins to decline.

1000 CE:
Northern Maya cities on the Yucatán Peninsula begin to be abandoned.

899 CE:
Tikal is abandoned.

(timeline continued)

1441 CE:
The lords of Xiu kill the ruler of Mayapan and burn the city.

1502:
Christopher Columbus encounters seagoing Maya traders.

1517:
Córdoba and his Spanish troops land on the beaches of the Yucatan. Native people are overwhelmed by European diseases of smallpox, flu, and measles. Over the next century, nine out of ten native people die from these diseases.

1519:
Hernán Cortés explores the Yucatan.

1562:
Fray Diego de Landa burns Maya artifacts and codices.

1847:
The Yucatan Maya once again rise up against the Mexican government.

1761: *Jacinto Canek leads the Maya on the Yucatan against the Spanish government.*

1952:
The tomb at Palenque is discovered and dug up by Mexican archaeologist Alberto Ruz. This is the first time a tomb is found inside a Maya pyramid.

1750

2000

1992:
Rigoberta Menchú Tum wins the Nobel Peace Prize for battling to save the Maya people of Guatemala.

1995:
The Guatemalan government formally ends repression of the Maya people.

2011:
An ancient Maya road is discovered near the Loma Caldera volcano, indicating a way for the Maya to escape during a volcanic eruption.

GLOSSARY

archaeologists (ahr-kee-AH-luh-jists) people who study the past, which often involves digging up old buildings, objects, and bones and examining them carefully

architects (AHR-ki-tekts) people who design buildings and supervise the way they are built

artifacts (AHR-tuh-fakts) objects made or changed by human beings, such as tools or weapons used in the past

artisans (AHR-tih-zuhnz) people who are skilled at working with their hands at particular crafts

breechcloths (BREECH-klawths) clothing worn around the loins and buttocks

caste (KAST) any class or group of society sharing common cultural features

cenotes (seh-NOH-tayz) sinkholes or naturally forming wells, formed by the collapse of surface limestone

codices (KOH-dih-sees) collections of manuscript pages held together by stitching or folding; an early form of books

dynasties (DYE-nuh-steez) series of rulers belonging to the same family

furrows (FUR-ohz) the long, narrow grooves that a plow cuts in the ground

glyphs (GLIFS) written symbols used to represent spoken words

guerrilla (guh-RIL-uh) a member of a small group of fighters or soldiers that often launches surprise attacks against an official army

hieroglyphics (hye-roh-GLIF-iks) a system of writing used by ancient Mayas, made up of pictures and symbols that stand for words and syllables

machete (muh-SHET-ee) a long, heavy knife with a broad blade, used as a tool or a weapon

Mesoamerica (mez-oh-uh-MARE-ih-kuh) the area extending from central Mexico south to Honduras and Nicaragua in which several pre-Columbian cultures thrived

murals (MYOOR-uhlz) large paintings done on a wall

pantheon (PAN-thee-ahn) the gods of a particular mythology grouped together

political (puh-LIT-i-kuhl) of or having to do with governments and how they are run

pyramids (PIR-uh-midz) ancient stone monuments where rulers and their treasures were buried and rituals were performed

rituals (RICH-oo-uhlz) acts or series of acts that are always performed in the same way, usually as part of a religious or social ceremony

sacrifices (SAK-ruh-fise-ez) the offerings of something to a god or other supernatural being

shamans (SHAY-muhnz) healer in some traditional societies who deal with beings in the spirit world

stelae (STEE-lahy) upright stone slabs or pillars bearing inscriptions or designs and serving as monuments or markers

tribute (TRIB-yoot) something done, given, or said to show thanks or respect, or to repay an obligation

FIND OUT MORE

BOOKS

Coulter, Laurie. *Ballplayers and Bonesetters: One Hundred Ancient Aztec and Maya Jobs You Might Have Adored or Abhorred*. Toronto: Annick Press, 2008.

Holm, Kirsten. *Everyday Life in the Maya Civilization*. New York: Rosen Publishing Group, 2012.

Menchú, Rigoberta. *The Honey Jar*. Toronto: Groundwood Books, 2006.

Perl, Lila. *The Ancient Maya*. New York: Franklin Watts, 2005.

Stray, Geoff. *The Mayan and Other Ancient Calendars*. New York: Walker & Co., 2007.

Visit this Scholastic Web site for more information on the Ancient Maya:
www.factsfornow.scholastic.com
Enter the keywords **Ancient Maya**

INDEX

Page numbers in *italics* indicate a photograph or map

(index continued)

ABOUT THE AUTHOR

Barbara Somervill has written more than 200 children's nonfiction books. She is fascinated by the Maya culture and has visited Chichen Itza and Tulum in the Yucatan. "Climbing up the great pyramid in Chichen Itza was incredibly difficult. It is 365 steps up and at a 45-degree angle—a long, hard climb. The view from the top is magnificent. You can see about 20 miles (32 km) in every direction on a clear day," she says. "One of the most interesting things about the Maya culture is that new information is being found every year."